THE TWO FRIDAS

Memories written by

Frida Kahlo

Illustrations:

Gianluca Folì

Schiffer**Kids**™

4880 Lower Valley Road, Atglen, PA 19310

I must have been six years old when I formed an intense imaginary friendship with a girl . . . who was more or less my age.

Standing at the window of what was then my room, which looked out onto Allende Street, I would fog up one of the bottom panes with my breath.
And with a finger I would draw a "door" . . .

In my imagination, I would go through that door, and with great joy and urgency, I would cross the flatland stretched out before me until I reached a creamery called PINZÓN . . .

I would dive in through the Ó in PINZÓN and TUMBLE down to the inside of the earth, where "my imaginary friend" was always waiting for me.

I don't remember what she looked like or what color she was, but I do know that she was happy. She laughed a lot without making a sound. She was nimble. And she danced as if she were weightless.

I would follow her every move, and while she danced, I would tell her my secret problems.

What problems? I don't remember. But she knew all about them just from listening to my voice . . .

When I would finally go back to the window, I would come in through the same door I had drawn on the glass.

When? How long had I been with "her"? I don't know. It could have been a second or thousands of years . . .

I was happy. I would wipe the "door" away with my hand and it would "disappear."

I would run with my secret and my joy to the farthest corner of the patio of my house, and, always in the same place, under a lemon verbena tree, I would shout and laugh, amazed to be alone with my great happiness and fresh memories of the girl.

It has been 34 years since I experienced that magical friendship, and every time I remember it, it is rekindled and grows more and more inside my world.

Pinzón, 1950. FRIDA KAHLO

More about Frida Kahlo

Frida is a very famous painter—possibly the most famous female painter in the world. Her paintings are unmistakable because her portrait appears in each one. This book revives a fragment of her diary, a memory of her childhood, which she wrote on ivory-colored pages full of ideas, doodles, drawings, and little anecdotes from her life. In this book, it is Frida Kahlo's words, rather than her paintings, that are the focus. Her story invites us to travel to Mexico, her native country, to her neighborhood, Coyoacán, one of the most beautiful areas in Mexico City, and to her house, the Blue House, a mansion that looks like a piece of heaven both inside and out. Frida was born there on July 6, 1907. There are lots of photos of her as a child with her older sisters, Matilde and Adriana, and her younger sister and playmate, Cristina. Her father, Guillermo Kahlo, was a photographer of German descent.

Magdalena Carmen Frida Kahlo Calderón.

The girls loved posing in colorful and flamboyant regional costumes that were full of lace crocheted by their mother, Matilde Calderón. Frida's childhood, however, also had terrible moments. Shortly after starting school, she contracted a terrible illness that affected her right leg. From then on, she had difficulty walking, but that didn't stop her from playing soccer with Cristina or from climbing trees. According to her diary, it was around the time of her illness that she discovered her imaginary friend. And this friend must have been very important because Frida never forgot her. She even dedicated a painting titled The Two Fridas to her in 1939.

"I paint flowers so they don't die."

"The most powerful art in life is to make pain a talisman that heals, a butterfly that is reborn flourished in a festival of colors."

Frida Kahlo is an icon for many artists.

Why did Frida almost always paint self-portraits? She explained why many times. As the result of a serious accident, Frida was bedridden for many days, months, and years. She painted while tucked in between the sheets, and she requested that a mirror be placed in front of her so that she could paint what she knew best: Frida. Her vocation as a painter grew along with her: everything she did, thought about, or loved was reflected in her work. She married Diego Rivera, another Mexican painter; she loved her country and her culture; and she fought for her ideals, for the freedom of men and women, for justice, and also for the beauty of life. She was a revolutionary woman. But before that, way before that, she was a little girl who had a magical, joyful, secret-filled friendship.

A te, Paola, mio biondo sole.
G. F.

Type set in P22Parrish/Adobe Garamond Pro
Editorial Direction: Fernando Diego García
Art Direction: Sebastián García Schnetzer
Edition: Estrella Borrego
Correction: Sara Díez Santidrián

ISBN: 978-0-7643-6116-6
Printed in China

Published by Schiffer Kids
An imprint of Schiffer Publishing, Ltd.
4880 Lower Valley Road
Atglen, PA 19310
Phone: (610) 593-1777; Fax: (610) 593-2002
E-mail: Info@schifferbooks.com
Web: www.schifferbooks.com

For our complete selection of fine books on this and related subjects, please visit our website at www.schifferbooks.com. You may also write for a free catalog.

Schiffer Publishing's titles are available at special discounts for bulk purchases for sales promotions or premiums. Special editions, including personalized covers, corporate imprints, and excerpts, can be created in large quantities for special needs. For more information, contact the publisher.

We are always looking for people to write books on new and related subjects. If you have an idea for a book, please contact us at proposals@schifferbooks.com.